William Langton

Sonnets Original and Translations from the Italian

William Langton

Sonnets Original and Translations from the Italian

ISBN/EAN: 9783337230883

Printed in Europe, USA, Canada, Australia, Japan

Cover: Foto ©Thomas Meinert / pixelio.de

More available books at **www.hansebooks.com**

SONNETS

ORIGINAL AND

TRANSLATIONS FROM THE ITALIAN

BY

WILLIAM LANGTON

WITH PORTRAITS AND A NOTICE OF HIS LIFE

PRINTED FOR PRIVATE CIRCULATION BY ONE OF HIS DAUGHTERS

Manchester

J. E. CORNISH, 16 ST. ANN'S SQUARE

1897

CONTENTS

WILLIAM LANGTON (1803–1881), antiquary and financier, son of Thomas Langton of Kirkham (who died in 1838 in Canada West), was born at Farfield near Addingham, in the West Riding of Yorkshire, on 17th April 1803. His mother was the daughter of the Rev. William Currer, Vicar of Clapham, Yorkshire. He was educated chiefly on the Continent, in Switzerland, Italy, and Germany, in which countries the family resided for some years, and where he acquired familiarity with foreign languages. For a short time he was a pupil of Pestalozzi at Yverdun, in whose career and system of education his father was greatly interested. From 1821 to 1829 he was engaged in business in Liverpool, during the latter part of the time as agent for some mercantile firms in Russia. In August 1829 he accepted a responsible position in Messrs. Heywood's bank in Manchester, and in connection with that house he continued until 1854, when he became managing director of the Manchester and Salford Bank, which grew and flourished under his rule for the next twenty-two years. He resigned in October 1876 in consequence of the complete failure of his sight.

During the long period of his residence in Manchester he was justly regarded as one of its most accomplished and philanthropic citizens, and was associated in the establishment of some of its prominent institutions. He took a leading part in the projection of the Manchester Athenæum in 1836. His services were publicly recognised in 1881 by the presentation to the Athenæum of his marble medallion bust, along with those of his co-founders, Richard Cobden and James Heywood, F.R.S. When the Chetham Society was founded in 1843 he became one of its earliest members, and was elected its treasurer, subsequently exchanging that office for the honorary secretaryship. He edited for the Society three volumes of *Chetham Miscellanies*, 1851, 1856, and 1862; *Lancashire Inquisitions Post Mortem*, 1875; and *Benall's Visitation of Lancashire of 1533*, 2 vols., 1876-82. He was, in association with Dr. Kay, afterwards Sir J. P. Kay, Shuttleworth, a chief promoter of the Manchester "District Provident Society," 1833, and of the Manchester Statistical Society in the same year. To the latter Society he contributed in 1857 a paper on the "Balance of Account between the Mercantile Public and the Bank of England," and in 1867 a presidential address.

Among other professional papers he wrote "On Banks and Bank Shareholders," 1879, and a letter on Savings Banks, 1880, addressed to the Chancellor of the Exchequer.

He was an accurate genealogist, herald, and antiquary, a philologist, a skilful draughtsman, a musician, and a graceful writer of verse, both in his own language and in Italian.

He spent his retirement at Ingatestone in Essex, where he died on 29th September 1881. He was buried in Fryerning Churchyard, Essex.

He married, at Kirkham, Lancashire, on 15th November 1831, Margaret, daughter of Joseph Hornby of Ribby, Lancashire, and had issue three sons and six daughters.

SONNETS

SONNET ADDRESSED TO ALICE HORNBY (OF RIBBY, LANCASHIRE) ON HER BIRTHDAY

13TH SEPTEMBER 1829

As late I watch'd the orb which rules the night
    Riding triumphant through the azure sky,
And, with the chaste resplendence of her light,
    Outshining far the lesser fires on high,
Delighted fancy sped on pinions bright,
    And dwelt on Alice with enraptured eye;
For thus her beauty charms the wondering sight,
    Eclipsing every vain attempt to vie:
The swift revolving years with gifts abound
    Which grace thy features, and thy mind adorn,
    May'st thou on each succeeding natal morn
Dearer, as nearer, unto heaven be found;
And may He grant an overflowing chalice
Of peace to be thy lot on earth, sweet Alice.

B

MY BIRTHDAY

17TH APRIL 1877

ANOTHER landmark on life's road is passed,
    And still I toil along the weary way ;
    No longer blithe as in the early day,
For gloom of night looms o'er my path at last ;
The lengthening shadows o'er the landscape cast,
 . Give warning of the dangers of delay,
    Or lest our wandering steps be led astray,
When life's dull stream must needs be ebbing fast ;
How much that should be wrought remains undone !
    Why did I loiter fading flowers to cull ?
How great the guerdon that I might have won,
    When fruits which turn to ash I stay'd to pull !
For now that falls the night, and fails the breath,
We faint in darkness and the shades of death.

MY WEDDING DAY

15TH NOVEMBER 1876

FULL five times nine long years have pass'd away
   Since holy wedlock joined our hands in prayer,
   And though so many snows have bleach'd our hair,
The blood flows warmly through our hearts alway :
Of nine the Lord has given us in our day,
   Three we know safe in the good Shepherd's care,
   We thank Him also for the rest, who share
The joys and sorrows of our lengthening way.
Though toil of fifty years has left me blind,
   And anchorless now drift the aims of life,
Yet shall I seek to keep an even mind,
   Unmindful of external wrong and strife ;
May sweet domestic joys my solace prove,
Crown'd by the blessings of Faith, Hope and Love.

BLINDNESS

Upon the opening eye there strikes no ray
   Dispelling visions of the dreaming brain,
   Until by touch convinced they still remain
And reason slowly thus regains her sway.
By sound alone I hail returning day,
   To share its labours now I sigh in vain ;
   Terrors of darkness ever round me reign,
And eve and morn no conscious change betray ;
Thought fades in efforts to record its flow,
   And solitary hours oft run to waste,
The pride of independence is brought low ;
   Yet music of its charms is still possess'd,
The flowers their fragrance yield, the sun its glow,
   And fond affection fills the grateful breast.

   April 1877.

The expression "Terrors of darkness" having been criticised, it is vindicated in the following lines :—

"Qui ambulat in tenebris, nescit quo vadet."—JOHN xii. 35.

ONCE, overtaken by the shades of night,
  I rambled on a trackless mountain side,
  Sound of the distant wave my only guide
To point my course adown the dizzy height;
Hard too it was to place my steps aright
  Across a moorland dreary waste and wide,
  The view obscured by mist on every side,
No sign to mark the road, no star in sight;
      By day we spring from rock to rock, and wind
Our way through swamp and quagmire fearlessly,
  But though the darkness all these dangers screen,
    Our steps will be like footfall of the blind,
For the unknown we ever magnify,
    And who feels not the awe of the unseen?

July 1877.

SIC TRANSIT GLORIA MUNDI

THE light of day is fading e'er 'tis night,
   No more shall graceful forms enchant mine eye,
   The rainbow with its hues of tenderest dye,
The moon, the stars no longer yield delight,
The sunlit landscape gladdens not my sight,
   Its varied features I shall ne'er descry ;
   Shade of the grove and splendour of the sky,
No more may be discern'd for lack of light,
      Thus pass the glories of this sensuous world !
   So doth the final darkness o'er me loom,
Nearing the brink of the unknown abyss ;
      But by the eye of faith I see unfurl'd
   Christ's banner, through the portals of the tomb,
Leading a ransom'd host to realms of bliss.

MANCHESTER, *July* 1875.

PRAYER

Blind Bartimæus, by the passers by
    Coldly rebuked and bid to hold his peace,
    His prayer to Christ for mercy did not cease
Until the son of David heard his cry.
"What wouldest thou?" enquir'd our gracious Lord—
    "That sight I may receive"—the prompt reply;
    A gentle touch was laid on either eye,
And Bartimæus stood with sight restored!
Then did he follow where the Saviour led.
    Shut out, like him, from all the joys of day,
    That darkness be withdrawn, I too would pray,
Though Hope, last treasure of this life, is fled.
Lo! prayer is answered—"Live by Faith, not sight;
To follow Jesus ask for inward light."

April 1877.

NOR sun nor moon now guide my steps aright,

    Before my day of pilgrimage is past

    Darkness its shadow o'er my path has cast,

Where'er I gaze or wander all is night,

Conscious that earth is ever fair and bright,

    Teeming with life gift of the first and last,

    Moving through boundless space and splendour vast;

All teaches me to live by faith, not sight:

'Tis whisper'd in the stillness of the tomb,

    Through whose dark portal Christ hath led the way

To where the true Light shines in life to come.

    Light of the world! Source of eternal day!

To end in outer darkness were our doom

    Depriv'd of hope, enkindled by Thy ray.

January 1880.

FAITH holds the Cross to show how Jesus died,
    Giving to Hope her anchor's steadfast hold ;
    Of Charity the ample arms enfold
Sweet infant forms seen gathering to her side.
These Graces bless each home where they abide :
    Hope the assurance gives of joys untold,
    Which here the eyes of Faith alone behold,
To thought and sense an insight yet denied;
The boon of Charity is not concealed,
    'Tis felt beneath, around us, and above,
While milk of kindness tender fountains yield ;
    Such streams of healing and of mercy prove
Foretaste of heavenly bliss to earth revealed,
    Reflecting throughout time Christ's endless love.

EUGENIE DE GUÉRIN

(*Journal*, 20TH OCTOBER 1839, PAGE 294)

THIS tale I heard from lips of gentle maid :—
    " As through the fields my lingering steps I bent
    On living nature's wondrous works intent,
I marked a flower in glorious hues arrayed
On my return to cull, and onward sped ;
    But homeward by another way I went,
    And on the morrow fruitless efforts spent
To win my prize—the precious bloom was shed."
Hence learn, young wanderer on the path of life,
    When claims of sympathy beset thy way,
    That acts of mercy never brook delay.
Seize the occasion ere it be too late
The pangs of want or woe to mitigate,
To bind up wounds, or quell unholy strife.

How many unremember'd idle words,
 Impulsive acts done, counting not the cost,
 And sad neglects of old to memory lost,
Th' accusing angel in his book records!
Awaken'd conscience no content accords,
 For best designs oft-times by sin are cross'd.
 Unto frail man, like vessel tempest-toss'd,
The tide of life no resting-place affords.
O Lord of power and love! accept my prayer
 For those who do, and did me hurt, I plead,
But most for those I may have caus'd to err;
 Forgive our sins of thought, and word, and deed,
Confirm our hope that mercy we may share,
 For Faith assures that Christ doth intercede.

LIFE

May 1877

The restless waves, the hills, the sylvan glade,
　　The pathless moorland, and the devious way,
　　All various phases of our life portray ;
As dawn and noontide into twilight fade,
The cloudless calm, and then the havoc made
　　By wind and hail, when lurid lightnings play,
　　A picture of the human mind display,
By prudence guided, or by passion sway'd ;
Despair, like gloom of night in starless sky,
　　O'erwhelms the soul ; but sunshine reappears,
　　And wakening faith and hope the pilgrim cheers ;
Sorrows of life in breezes wail or sigh,
　　Heralds of joy, the songsters of the grove
　　Pour forth the strains of gratitude and love.

1878

HIS net the fisher weaves, then ploughs the deep,
    He draws the seine, and lands the shining spoil;
    The husbandman upturns the grateful soil,
Which soon repays the hands that sow and reap;
The roads to learning and renown are steep;
    'Tis labour fills our stores of wine and oil,
    Earth yields her gold but to the sons of toil,
Who hail returning day refreshed by sleep;
Success is not for those who scorn endeavour,
    Or having held the plough their hand withdraw.
" If any work not neither shall he eat,"
    For is not labour universal law?
Creation travaileth, as so 'tis meet,
Since the Eternal Father worketh ever.

DESIRE not worldly honours, pompous show!
    For as the breath of heaven is human fame,
    Which where it listeth blows, while whence it came,
And whither it doth tend, may no man know;
Yea! though thy head be sprinkled with the snow
    Of many winters—well spent, free from blame,
    In kindness rich—most surely will thy name
Be lost 'midst waves, which to oblivion flow.
When Jesus dwelt upon this earth and taught,
    He won the meek and lowly as His own,
    Asking His followers—"How can ye believe
Who each from other glory fain receive,
When in your blindness ye have never sought
    That honour which is gift of God alone?"

WHEN the bright orb of day has ceased to blaze,
    Eclipsing other splendours by his light,
    Countless we view the glories of the night,
While awe and wonder hold us as we gaze ;
Vainly we seek our thoughts on high to raise,
    And know the Lord's immeasurable might,
    'Tis asked if voice can reach to such a height
And why intone the hymn of prayer and praise ?
Scoffers bow down ! view in the world below
    The tender mercies of a Father's care,
The source from which unbounded blessings flow ;
    Seek but to find His finger everywhere,
From meanest reptile hides He not His face,
And sinful man He deigns to save by grace.

" Sperme mundem
Sperme te ipsum
Sperme sperme "

THE world with all its treasures in your eyes
    Should seem but dross, beauty and joy and fame
    The fleeting flicker of expiring flame,
And luxury the chief of vanities ;
Your wit and talents ever lightly prize,
    Humble yourselves to dust from whence ye came,
    And of your weakness glory in the shame,
Of all creation lords—yourselves despise ;
Scorn and contempt your gracious Master bore,
    The cup of bitterness He meekly drank ;
Ever His pattern keep your eyes before,
    And if like Him abased, oh ! learn to thank,
Of scoffs and gibes heed not the stinging voice,
When spurn'd, despis'd, rejected, then rejoice !

LORD! who shall come within Thy dwelling place?
   Or who shall rest upon Thy holy hill?
   Ev'n he who seeks with truth to do Thy will,
And run in purity th' appointed race,
Out of whose heart proceedeth nothing base,
   Who never speaketh of his neighbour ill,
   Those chiding who Thy law do not fulfil,
Revering all who bow before Thy face,
Who when he lendeth seeketh not for gain,
   Who takes no mean advantage of the frail,
      Who when to brother man his faith he plights,
To his own hindrance doth his troth maintain;
   Such is the man whose cause shall never fail,
      Such is the man in whom the Lord delights.

C

PSALM XXIII

Nought can I lack, my Shepherd is the Lord,
 Me He doth ever in green pastures feed,
 When fainting to refreshing waters lead,
And for my wandering steps a guide accord ;
To find the path of righteousness His word
 Supplies true light for those who meekly read ;
 There wells of comfort spring to meet our need,
There living thought sweet nourishment afford ;
 Yea though I wander through the vale of death,
And shades of night surround my sinking soul,
 On His support I firmly rest my faith ;
The Lord by His anointing maketh whole,
 Strength He vouchsafeth by His staff and rod ;
 No ill I fear in presence of my God

IN youth we crave for knowledge; older grown,
    Desires of wealth, power, fame our spirits move
    To toil for what delusive phantoms prove,
Frail fabrics fated to be overthrown;
Each earthly treasure counts but as a loan,
    In mercy granted by the Lord above,
    Parents, or spouse, or offspring of our love,
Dear beyond price, yet are they not our own,
These all will leave us, or by us be left
    For regions where temptation, sin, and shame
        No entrance find, and sorrow hath no place;
Grieve not as if ye were of hope bereft,
    How can the blest of tears a tribute claim,
        When angels waft them to the throne of grace?

" For I am the Lord, I change not."—MAL. iii. 6.

1879

YOUTH into manhood grown soon fades in age ;
  The end of strength and beauty is decay ;
  Season succeeds to season, night to day,
And calm precedes the surging billow's rage ;
The rise and fall of power fill history's page,
  Now bright with peace, now soiled with savage fray ;
  Sorrow and joy oft hold alternate sway,
While good and ill mysterious warfare wage ;
Unchanged, unchangeable 'midst ceaseless change,
  The countless atoms, and the boundless spheres,
Obedient to God's loving mandate range ;
  Ungrateful man alone rebels and fears,
Wreck'd without hope, yet sav'd by grace at last,
If Faith's sure anchor on His Christ be cast.

A TRILOGY

YOUTH—MANHOOD—AGE

YOUTH

WE enter life as through a tangled wood,
   To our enquiring eyes no path in view,
   The signs to guide our progress slight and few ;
For shadows o'er the closing distance brood,
Our wandering steps we bend in faltering mood,
   To thread the labyrinth we need a clue,
   Without a guide of certain hand and true,
We fail in strength, we faint for lack of food ;
But heaven in mercy gave the parent's heart
   To lend support and find the narrow way,
The fruit of ripe experience to impart,
   Reclaiming erring steps when led astray ;
While Hope, sweet Christian grace, with cheering smiles,
And gleams of light, the weary way beguiles.

MANHOOD

FORTH from the thicket passing to the strand,
    A vast expanse of water meets the gaze,
    Whose bright horizon, gleaming through the haze,
Lures manhood on, tells of a golden land,
While some may sport, or sweep with nets the sand,
    These ply the oar, the swelling canvas raise,
    Scorning inglorious ease, luxurious days ;
Fame or ambition fires the sturdy band ;
Barren of fruit or rich with laden gain,
    The bark returning dances on the wave,
When tempest-toss'd upheaves the yeasty main,
    Mercy Divine alike may wreck or save ;
This thought nerves hearts 'midst elemental strife,
Faith teaching death to be but birth of life.

AGE

SAV'D from the perils of the groaning sea
    We grasp the rock, we scale the mountain side,
    Trusting the path to rest and peace may guide,
And on the top we bend the grateful knee,
We higher rise, a higher still we see,
    The view grows ever wider and more wide ;
    'Tis well for age upon these heights to bide,
They point, O Lord, the way to heaven and Thee ;
Unto the mountain Christ withdrew and pray'd,
    'Twas there the chosen three His glory saw,
    The burning bush, the terrors of the law,
The promised land, all were from thence display'd,
    There spake the still small voice, which, from above,
    Yet whispers to the soul "My reign is Love."

SONNETS

ON THE MOTTO OF THE PETRE FAMILY

"SANS DIEU RIEN"

1878 AND 1880

Our Father! reigning in the heaven above,
 Be Thy pure law upheld in every heart!
 To each and all the bread of life impart;
Convinced of sin we would Thy mercy move,
The wrongs we suffer pardoning in love,
 So in redemption we may have our part;
 Bid from our path the evil one depart,
Lest his temptation our destruction prove;
Thus taught our Saviour Christ mankind to claim
 The common Fatherhood of God, when nigh
  We draw unto His throne, and meekly plead,
Invoking grace through Jesus' holy name;
 Without a Father in the Lord most high,
  Where were man's refuge in his hour of need?

THE babe reposing on a mother's breast

    The earliest dawn of sympathy portrays,

    And prattling childhood in its mimic plays

Of social instincts points the growing zest ;

The schoolmate friend becomes the honour'd guest

    Of the sweet home, where early love we trace

    Enthron'd supreme in matrimonial grace ;

With tender hopeful olive-branches blest,

The father's heart yearneth for trust and love,

    His offspring's weal an ever present thought ;

    Christ bade His followers claim this tender tie

When pleading with the Lord of Heaven above,

    He taught the Fatherhood of the most High ;

    Then if not sons of God we count as nought.

THROUGH pathless wastes the shepherd guides his sheep
　　To pasture rich refreshed by purling brook,
　　The fold he builds in quiet sheltered nook,
And scares the prowling wolves which round it creep;
So doth our Shepherd, Christ, His people keep
　　By the rich nurture of His sacred book,
　　And guards from evil, pointing by His crook
The heavenward way, oft rugged, strait, and steep;
Jesus! Thy sheep are widely folded now,
　　Devious their tracks in many pastures fed,
Still are they Thine, for by Thy word we know
　　One flock there shall be, by one Shepherd led;
Good Shepherd! guide us by Thy staff and rod,
All is as nought without Thee! Lord and God!

MYSTERIOUS mother! genial nature thou,
    In ever-varied glories art displayed,
    Whether with verdure be the plains arrayed,
Or snows repose upon the mountain's brow,
Or when the lurid lightnings overthrow
    The ancient monarchs of the wooded glade,
    And storms their terrors o'er the ocean spread,
      Before Thy majesty our heads we bow ;
Thy showers and streams refresh the thirsty land,
    Thy smiles upon the glowing harvest shine,
No foul miasma may thy storms withstand,
    Thy gifts are health, with stores of corn and wine,
Nothing if not obeying God's command,
    Ever the handmaid of a will Divine.

THE ceaseless order of returning day
    A wealth of life discloses to our view,
    In rich variety of form and hue,
Charming our senses wheresoe'er we stray ;
Earth, air, and water, each and all display
    Of living nature wonders old and new,
    And these the sentient soul with faith imbue
In an omnipotent Creator's sway ;
    Eclips'd the solar beams, mysterious night
Unveils of shining orbs a boundless field,
    To mortals forecast of the infinite ;
Blind ! now these glories are from me concealed ;
    Oh, bless the Lord who gave the sense of sight,
Without our God no light can be revealed.

WHEN nature's beauteous face is veiled in night,
   Unnumbered glories burst upon the eye,
   Which vainly seeks their limits to descry;
So when refracted doth the solar light
Give rays too delicate for human sight;
   Sounds too are made by footsteps of a fly,
   Whose wavelets the unaided ear defy;
Unfelt, unseen, and noiseless in their flight,
Monads in myriads fill the ambient air,
   And in the ocean's trackless depths abound;
May not ethereal beings everywhere
   Unseen, unheard, unfelt, our path surround?
Hail them as messengers from heaven above,
For nothing lives but by God's law of love.

In springtide, early morning of the year,
    Response is given to balmy breeze and shower
    By swelling bud, and opening leaf and flower,
Summer and autumn noontide radiance wear,
Gilding the crops which hill and valley bear,
    While blush the fruits 'neath genial solar power,
    Then rests in winter's sleep each leafless bower,
As calmly conscious of revival near ;
Works of the Lord ! Lo ! how ye praise the Lord,
    Speechless, yet teaching gratitude and trust ;
    Frail man ! to higher life called from the dust,
Taught and redeemèd by th' Incarnate Word,
    Repent and turn to God in praise and prayer,
    For nothing lives without His fostering care.

D

POWERS in ceaseless flow this globe surround,
 To guide whose streams men not in vain aspire,
 Light emanates with heat from orbs of fire,
By force unseen the universe is bound ;
Where'er we gaze, above, below, around,
 Wonders with awe the sentient soul inspire,
 Leading each heart to worship and admire,
Beauty and grace in nature's gifts abound ;
For life and health and for the teeming earth,
 Time and the seasons measured by its course,
For mind, and all to which the mind gives birth,
 We thank the Great Creator as the source
Whence Faith, Hope, Love, our highest blessings flow,
For without God we nothing have or know.

A BOUNDLESS field of labour and delight
They find who study life's instructive page,
Tracing its course in time from age to age,
Straying through flowery vale o'er wooded height;
The fishes sport, birds warble in their flight,
Yet all in internecine strife engage,
Whilst life and death incessant warfare wage;
So hath decreed the Lord of life and light;
To trace the origin of life on earth
The visionary sage essays in vain,
No life he finds but what in life had birth,
For man a mystery 'twill e'er remain,
'Tis His who ever shall be, is, and was;
Nought lives or lived without Thee, First Great Cause !

WE feel the winds of heaven now soft now keen,
    The waves of sound yield ever new delight,
    By fragrance flowers sweet sense of joy excite ;
Doubt we these powers because their force unseen ?
Blind to the charms of every earthly scene,
    A gracious answer to my prayer for light
    Is gently whisper'd : Live by faith not sight,
Trust not thyself, but on the Saviour lean ;
To man how limited the senses given,
    And when of finest temper prone to fail,
Reason, the best, the noblest gift of heaven,
    Its empire holdeth by a tenure frail,
All here is mystery ; life, memory, thought,
God above all ; without Him all is nought.

O'ER southern seas the shimmering sky displays
   A mimic scene of groves and stately piles,
So, on the trackless waste, delusive haze
   With sheen of meres the parchèd Arab wiles,
   A phantom light the weary wight beguiles,
For treacherous swamps he leaves the beaten ways;
Oft too vain hope the ardent youth betrays,
   Misled by fickle fortune's early smiles;
Who has not seen tinted by early dawn
   Across the glassy lake green pastures reach?
Then gentle winds breathe o'er the liquid lawn,
   Which shows the rugged margin of the beach;
A mocking spirit oft distorts our view,
Without our God we nothing know as true.

YIELDING to vain devices of the heart
    The patriarchs fell ; so in the sacred page
    'Tis writ ; and this has been in every age
The fate of those who from their God depart ;
Oh ! watch and pray the Spirit to impart,
    When ye in conflict with the world engage,
    Strength to stand firm when boiling passions rage,
To choose in devious ways the better part ;
Our God hath spoken, may His holy word
    Prove bread of life, the everlasting food
    For sinners ransomed by Christ's precious blood ;
Grant us to feel the presence of our Lord,
    In whom we have our being, move, and live,
    Without whose grace frail man may nought achieve.

PRIDE not thyself on accident of birth,

    The empty heirloom of historic name ;

    Covet not honours, title, wealth, or fame ;

Waste not thy precious life in festive mirth ;

If in thy transient pilgrimage on earth

    To do the will of God thy earnest aim,

    Shrink never through the sense of doubt or shame,

For envy ever dogs the steps of worth ; ·

He who hath wrought thee wrong is sure to hate,

    And malice prompts the ever ready lie,

If sport of evil tongues should be thy fate,

    Learn to forgive, and calumny defy ;

Dissemble not thy sins ! repent ! amend !

Lost without Christ as Saviour, Judge, and Friend.

THY gifts to man, O Lord, how manifold !
   Thy Holy Spirit where He listeth breathes;
   To whom with fire He toucheth, He bequeaths
Powers till then unknown, and might untold ;
Confronting stripes and death some makes He bold
   To win, as martyr'd saints, immortal wreaths;
   In other breasts the restless heart's blood seethes,
Prompting prophetic visions to unfold ;
Knowledge, discernment, wisdom, and the force
   Of fervent words, come to us from above,
   Gifts of the Spirit of Eternal Love,
As doth our faith, of peace and joy the source ;
   Into this toiling world we nothing brought,
   And without Thee, O God ! possess we nought.

LIFE'S journey drawing gently towards its close,
    Our toil-worn footsteps linger on the plain,
    Each rugged path entails a greater strain,
While dark and drear the narrowing landscape grows ;
Though waning light on wearied limbs impose
    For each unfinished task unwonted pain ;
    Forbid it, Lord ! while any powers remain,
That they be wasted idly in repose,
As are my days so be the promised strength,
    Till called to meet the universal doom ;
Sin can no more defile us when at length,
    Our labours o'er, we sleep within the tomb,
Cleansed in the blood of Christ, our risen Lord,
Nothing we fear while resting on His word.

" THERE is no God," the thoughtless fool hath said.
  Is there no God?   Behold Him everywhere,
  Upholding all things with a Father's care ;
Countless the creatures by His bounty fed,
Boundless in heaven's expanse His glories spread.
  Conscience He gives His judgments to declare,
  Yet deigns to hear the suppliant sinner's prayer,
And balm of comfort on his soul to shed.
Lord, what is man, that him Thou should'st regard ?
  Yet, 'tis in man that Thou art manifest.
  In Christ we know Thee, and in Him are blessed,
Enjoying in His service our reward ;
  Grant us the strength to follow at His call,
  And grace to feel that God is all in all !

GRANBATTISTA COTTA

AN ENGLISH VERSION—JAN. 1874

IN his fond heart oft-times the fool hath said :
  "There is no God who may the worlds uphold."
  Whether there be a God let him behold,
Tearing the impious veil from off his head !
Is there no God ? lo ! how the heavens are spread,
  Which to his blindness countless light unfold,
  Let him survey himself, and thus be told
By whose wise hand so wonderfully made ;
Is there no God ? Observe the crystal spring,
     The air we breathe, the soil whereon we dwell,
    The flower, the fruit, the rock, the wave, the breeze,
     In signs how eloquent of God they tell !
The Great First Cause we trace in everything,
  If faithless still, look forth and learn from these !

TRANSLATIONS FROM THE ITALIAN

SONNETS BY PETRARCA

SONETTO

THOUGHT soared with me aloft in heavenward flight,
    Where her I found, sought upon earth in vain,
    Dwelling with those whom the third heavens contain.
Less haughty now, in beauty yet more bright.
She took my hand, and said : in realms of light,
    If hope deceive not, we shall meet again.
    'Twas I on earth who caused thee so much pain,
Whose day was closed before the fall of night.
My bliss exceeds the grasp of human mind,
    I wait but thee, and that so much thy love
My graceful veil left in the tomb behind.
    Why did she cease? and why her hand remove?
For at the sound of words so pure and kind
    Well nigh had I remained in heaven above.

SONETTO

LXX

'Tis told that Cæsar, when that honoured head
   Was sent him by the traitor of the Nile,
   Tho' filled with sweet joy, in subtle guile,
A flood of tears before his followers shed.
And when the fate of war dismay had spread
   Amongst the people, Hannibal the while,
   Despite his country's woes, was seen to smile,
Smothering the care which on his spirit weighed.
So haps it that when bursts of passion rise,
   'Tis sought o'er them a veiling cloak to fling,
Changing its hues to favour a disguise.
   So if perchance I sometimes laugh or sing,
'Tis because thus the only means I find
To hide the tearful anguish of my mind.

SONETTO

LXXXIX

SWEET little bird ! who, singing in thy flight,
    Perchance lamented over days gone by,
    O'erwhelmed with darkness and the wintry sky,
Bereft of daylight, and of seasons bright ;
If as thou know'st thine own sad griefs aright,
    So also my sore cares thou could'st descry ;
    To this bereaved bosom thou should'st fly,
And share the anguish of its doleful plight ;
I wot not if our woes we share alike,
    As she thy mourn'd companion yet may live,
Me have both death and heaven combined to strike ;
    The season and the hour no comfort give,
Yet memories sweet or sad I would with thee
Discourse, sure of thy tender sympathy.

TRANSLATIONS FROM THE ITALIAN

OF

SONNETS BY VITTORIA COLONNA

RIME VARIE

RIME VARIE

I.—ELEGIAC

SOFTLY to vent my inward griefs I write
    (Griefs which the heart with holy light inflame),
    And not to give my glorious sun fresh flame,
Or praise to honoured dust and spirit bright.
Causes more just my woful plaints incite,
    I grieve to think I might impair his fame,
    'Tis meet from death to rescue his great name,
That other tongue should wiser words indite—
Faith, love and grief excuse my heavy moan,
    Time, even faith, and reason vainly tries
To lull my anguish.   Bitter tears alone,
    No sweet melodious song—deep glowing sighs,
No tender voice.—They on my verse bestow
No glory, but a halo o'er my woe.

RIME VARIE

XVII

GAZING from this loved rock there greets my sight,
  In rosy dawn, th' expanse of earth and heaven,
  And many phantoms from the heart are driven,
As mist unveils the view to day's sweet light
Thought rises with the sun to noontide height;
  So my rapt soul is led from morn till eve
Towards Him to whom more brilliant rays are given,
Who lures me to His home so fair and bright;
  Though not in heavenly chariot as once
  Midst flames of fire Elias to the sky,
Yet doth He seem in His own blaze to come,
  While doating fancy feigns that from on high
He bids me leave this lowly vale of woe,
And warms my soul with beatific glow

TRANSLATIONS FROM THE ITALIAN

OF

SONNETS BY VITTORIA COLONNA

RIME SACRE E MORALI

RIME SACRE E MORALI

XIX

Oh that my soul by living faith might see
    With how much love God did this world create,
    With how great price redeem ; and how ingrate
For tender mercies high as these are we !
How He sustains us from His treasury,
    How He vouchsafeth gifts, rich, rare, and great,
    How shields the sons in Him regenerate,
And chiefly those who trust most lovingly—
How from His everlasting throne above,
    When the strong warrior He doth crown and grace,
He arms and fires him with new sense of love—
    Yea ! though my thoughts reach no exalted place,
By mine own frailty weighed down so low,
How He forgives us, leastwise would I know.

RIME SACRE E MORALI

XXXI

ETERNAL Father! if by quickening grace
 A living branch am I of that true Vine
 Whose ample tendrils the whole earth entwine
  (Reckoned to me my faith for righteousness),
When o'er my growth dark shades the light efface,
 Thy heavenly eye beholdeth how I pine.
 If an undying spring in vain should shine,
And on the wither'd shoots no leaves replace,
Dress me, and train, that, grown to Thee more near,
 Thou e'er may'st feed me with Thy Holy Dew,
My roots refreshing with each falling tear.
 Sure is Thy pledge to stay me! Thou art true!
Come then, O Lord! so may I bear through Thee
Fruit sweet and worthy of so loved a Tree.

XLIX

THE Eye Divine, by its all-seeing power,
    The past and future in the present blends,
    To fervent hearts its light in mercy sends,
Nor lets cold doubts upon our spirits lower;
Our words, thoughts, works, and faith at every hour
    Before His vision ever stand revealed;
    Never the inward mind may be concealed,
However wily or however dour;
Securely resting on His promised grace,
    Why veil our sins, or blame on others throw,
Like the first parents of our fallen race?
    Rather we rend the cloak of outward show,
Unbosom to our Lord the secret soul,
And in His converse seek to be made whole.

RIME SACRE E MORALI

CXXIII

OVER His heart He felt cold shudder creep
  When in the garden; on His Father's name,
  To spare the anguish of His mortal frame,
He called: then on His followers, lost in sleep,
With looks of love He gazed, and sorrow deep.
  For ardent zeal on earth was now grown tame,
  And Heaven alone was heedful of His shame,
And the salvation we thereby do reap.
Therefore that slothful earth might now awake
  He straight resumed the ardour of His life;
And, like to one who high resolve doth take,
  Went forth again to mingle in the strife;
So from His friends their slumbers might be riven,
And holy death appease offended Heaven.

CXLIV

DESCERNING in my life such grave offence,
    Abashed, I seek from God my face to hide,
    And, unto Him who once for sinners died
Upon the tree, I turn with faith intense.
From primal, and from present wrath defence,
    His love and precious wounds for me provide ;
    For His rich promise hope and joy abide,
And banish abject fear and dire suspense ;
Thus did He pray when His last hour drew near :
    "O Father, grant that who on Me believe
    As one with us in heaven shall ever live."
Faithful in Christ, no dread my soul can feel,
Cleansed from its guilt in the consuming zeal
    Which moved Him on the cross for men to die.

CXLV

How can we feel in promises divine
   A living hope, if fear be e'er allowed
   Our hearts as with a chilling mist to shroud,
Preventing thus that glowing torch to shine?
And how can faith in the true light enshrine
   The joys which live, the works with love endowed,
   When oft our abject griefs, like envious cloud,
To dim the glorious reign of peace combine?
Over fair nature's face dark shadows move,
     Which as their causes vary, flit or rest,
   Rendering the gleams of sunshine yet more bright;
So may the virtues and the works of love,
   Mingling with Hope and Faith in heavenly light,
     'Midst doubts and griefs, irradiate the breast!

RIME SACRE E MORALI

CLXXVIII

As clustering Ivy, when by storm or fire
    Torn from its prop, seeks ever, but in vain,
    Writhing on earth, aloft to rise again—
So doth the soul, while grovelling in the mire
Of earth-born thoughts, fret with a wild desire
    The mark of its high calling to regain;
    For mean and scant are human minds to attain
The end which is its nature's true aspire;
While it neglects the sacred Tree to infold,
    Whose arms outspread still woo us to our weal,
Yielding from root to topmost spray firm hold,
    For so the Father wills the breach to heal;
Sole sure support ordains the cross shall prove,
And thus re-knits the precious bonds of love.

RIME SACRE E MORALI

CLXXIX

SEND to my heart even now, O blessed Lord!
　　Of burning faith a ray so fresh and clear
　　That Thy whole will may grow to me more dear;
As I would serve for love, not for reward.
No bitter drop Thy soothing springs afford,
　　Whether they meet the eye, or greet the ear;
　　In beauty clothed do all Thy works appear,
Most bounteous when Thou seem'st the least to accord.
If, as Thy servant, I a boon might crave,
　　This faith would I possess, to warm and shine,
　　And ever feed the soul with light Divine.
Virtue from Thee goes forth, and if it gave
　　To roots deep planted a firm hold in me,
　　Much loving fruit I might return to Thee.

CXCIV

NOT here the shepherds, nor this lowly place,
    Nor of yon ancient man the pious love,
    Nor sweet angelic voices from above,
Nor the blest virgin mother's fond embrace,
Nor the wise kings, who, from a jewelled case,
    Pour precious gifts with balms from spicy grove,
    But source of honour Thou to them didst prove
In the true homage of Thine act of grace.
I know that Thou true God, as man then born,
    Still dwellest here, therefore I envy none;
Not that I came so late makes me to mourn,
Nor that I find the present age forlorn;
But woe to me! my faith burns not so bright
As theirs, who saw Thee in that dawn of light.

"CHE COSA È VERITÀ?"

DEI suoi calmò le anime paurose,
    Mostrandogli le man, i piedi, il lato,
    Il dubbio non ripreso, ma quetato
Di lui, che il dito nelle piaghe pose.
Ma quando fe' richieste presuntuose
    Nel tribunal, il giúdice spietato,
    E per schermir disse a Gesù Pilato
"Che cosa è Veritade?" non rispose.
Dev' io temer i dubbi confessare,
    Cercando il falso sciogliere dal vero,
La legge tua sperando imparare,
    Seguendo il lume con desir sincero?
Deh, vieni Spirito dell' Eterno Amore!
Di speme e fede ognor empiendo il cuore.

"WHAT IS TRUTH?"

THE blest, who walked with Christ and heard His word,
    By Him were shown His wounded limbs and side;
    And one who doubted still He did not chide,
But further proof of touch He deign'd afford.
Then was He hail'd with fervour "God and Lord!"
    But when the judge asked, "What is Truth?" in pride
    Of place and power the victim to deride,
He to the taunt no answer would accord;
Since hard the task to part the false and true.
    Will honest doubt the Father e'er reprove
In those who earnestly the light pursue,
    And find in all His works a law of love?
Oh come, then, Holy Spirit, and in ruth
Illume our hearts and teach us "What is Truth."

PALLIDA giace ; ma non meno bella
Che qualora arrossendo la mirai ;
La fronte non s' attrista agli altrui guai ;
Nessuno sorriso le sue labbra abbella ;
Non s' ode più la soave sua favella ;
Degli occhi estinti sono i vaghi rai
E pio sospir non muove il seno omai ;
Di lei l' imago vi è : ma non è quella
Che con almo fiato di spirto vivo
In me svegliò desir di nuova vita.
Tanto valor dov' é ? Quel colpo fiero
Mortal mi lascia d' ogni gioja privo :
Ma guardo in alto donde viene aita
E perchè sempre amando credo e spero.

"So coldly sweet, so deadly fair!
We start! for soul is wanting there."—BYRON.

TRANSLATION

THAT shrouded form (when living not more fair)
    I watched, as in the silent room she lay,
    No gentle smiles on those pale lips now play,
The brow no longer tells of tender care,
The voice is hushed, Ah! once so sweet in prayer!
    No blush, no sigh unspoken thoughts betray,
    From the glaz'd eye there speeds no quickening ray,
'Tis but her effigy! she is not there!
The mind inspiring soul, the genial breath
    Which glow of higher life within me fann'd
Fled! whither fled?   By that fell stroke of death
    Faith, hope, and joy from my sad heart seem bann'd.
Yet no! I doubt no more, for still I love,
And Hope assurance gives of life above.

January 1873.

TRANSLATION

Graziella, the Neapolitan fisherman's daughter.—LAMARTINE.
"In every age the mantle of life and death, who is kinder as
well as wiser than we are, has transplanted to heaven young earth's
sweetest flower."
>"Ich habe genossen das irdische Glück,
>Ich habe gelebt und geliebt."—SCHILLER.

"INNATELY modest, innocently brave,
   Unskill'd to veil the language of her eyes,
   Guileless of speech, too truthful to be wise,
Pious as those who plough the fitful wave
Trusting the saints their fragile bark to save,
   Pure as the blue serene of southern skies,
   Knowing no sin in love, she scorn'd disguise,
And found the haven of an early grave.
Near thee will ever tarry love, my soul."
   Over the life of him who told the tale,
These dying words a living influence proved,
The spell which bound her rules from pole to pole.
   Mourn her no more, ye maidens! cease to wail!
Earth's greatest bliss was hers, she lived and loved.

THE PET LAMB

A true Tale of Canadian Life

(Written for K. M. Greenwood)

FABLES are writ a moral to infold ;
But truth is often stranger when 'tis told
Than even fiction of distemper'd brain.
The tale I tell is true, the moral plain.
Bereft by misadventure of its dam,
We, to our homestead, took the orphan lamb ;
He never missed a mother's tender care,
For loving sympathetic hearts were there,
Each vying with the others to afford
Whatever were his wants of bed and board ;
The very dogs which roamed within the yard
Treated the helpless pet with kind regard,
And as he grew to be both strong and brisk,
As it is wont, the lamb began to frisk,
Joining in play and gambols without end—

Our great newfoundland, the lamb's special friend,
Would seize him by his wool, and shake him soundly,
When, in return, the lamb would butt him roundly.
The lamb now made himself too much at home,
Upstairs and downstairs he would boldly roam—
Intruding in his rambles into places,
Unwelcome guest! he sank in the good graces
Of maid and mistress. Thus his doom was sealed,
His proper place they said was in the field.
A neighbouring farmer owned a flock of sheep,
So him we urged our banished pet to keep.
Condemned to part, uprose a great lament;
But tears were dried, and off the lamb was sent.
Now as I tell my tale truth must be spoken:
Habits contracted are but rarely broken;
In comrades new the lamb no pleasure took,
And for the dogs the fleecy flock forsook;
And when, one morn, a prowling wolf drew nigh,
And dogs gave chase, he joined the hue and cry.
Canadian wolves are cowards; but e'en they,
When sorely pressed, will turn and stand at bay,
And then their deadly fangs the dogs affright,
Who, in their turn, turn tail and take to flight.
So did it hap, I trow, upon that day :—
Their duty done, the wolf now driven away,

The dogs returned, each looking mighty clever,
Our friend, the lamb, alas! returnèd—never.

MORAL

A Latin proverb which I heard in youth,
Propounds as Nature's law the wholesome truth
That like with like are apt to congregate.
The moral of the tale which I relate
Shows that to deviate from Nature's course,
Of woe unseen may be the fatal source;
Warns not to roam beyond our native spheres,
Nor shun in life foregathering with our peers;
Teaches that habits in our youth contracted,
Rarely in after life are counteracted.

DOCKLANDS, *July* 1878.

DREAMS SLEEPING AND WAKING

PART I

MUCH spent and worn I laid me on my bed,
    And gentle sleep, the friend of the distress'd,
    Came at my call, and that most blessed guest
His soothing influence o'er my spirit shed.
Anon I dream'd and thought I heard a tread
    Draw nigh; but I, with weariness oppress'd,
    Bade it be gone, and not disturb my rest.
At last, a hand was laid upon my head;
"Who is it?" with a troubled voice I cried,
    But all impatience soon to joy gave place,
"It is your mother!" softly was replied.

    Of sleep or languor now there seem'd no trace,
I started up: my arms flew open wide,
And closed in one long passionate embrace.

Part II

"My mother!" cried I—but my dream was gone!
 Like other joys of earth it would not stay;
 The loved one faded from my arms away,
And I, once more, was on my couch alone.
But of that well-known voice the tender tone
 Still seem'd to linger with me all the day;
 And I could fancy that perhaps it may
Rouse me again when, life's long journey done,
I sleep in death: may not Eternal Love,
 Aye on His children's happiness intent,
Lest, 'midst the glories of the world above,
 Our weakness suffer strange bewilderment,
Send those to wake us who erst gave us birth,
Or other of our best beloved on earth?

ANNE LANGTON.

THE END

Printed by R. & R. CLARK, LIMITED, *Edinburgh.*

www.ingramcontent.com/pod-product-compliance
Lightning Source LLC
Chambersburg PA
CBHW020306090426
42735CB00009B/1232